GU01018974

3) Put the hot bit of the iron firmly upon the joint and allow a few seconds for the joint to heat up.
Take care. The soldering iron bit and metal shaft can burn the skin!

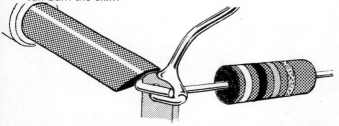

4) Lightly push the end of the solder onto the joint and allow the solder to flow freely over the whole joint. DO NOT apply the solder to the bit, the heat of the joint should do the melting.

5) Allow the solder to cool until it goes solid.

GOOD SOLDER JOINTS should be bright and shiny, if the joint looks very dull and grey it may be a bad joint, called a DRY JOINT. If this is so, remake the joint.
Components are usually soldered to copper tags. It is possible to replace the screw cups of the radio with small copper nails and solder the components onto these. Wrap the wires around the nail before soldering so that the joint is made firm.

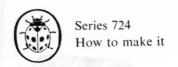

Series 724
How to make it

With superb colour diagrams and an equally easy-to-follow text, this fascinating book shows how to make a transistor radio capable of receiving a number of stations.

First to be described is a simple crystal set that really works. Stage-by-stage the set is added to (each stage a complete working radio) until a powerful transistor radio is completed.

Easily, inexpensively, and learning as you go, as each section is added you will experience the thrill, shared by all radio constructors, of listening to sounds coming from a radio receiver that is your own work.

A Ladybird 'How to make it' book

making a
Transistor Radio

by G. C. DOBBS

with illustrations by B. H. ROBINSON

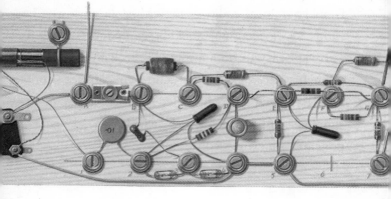

Publishers: Ladybird Books Ltd . Loughborough
© Ladybird Books Ltd (formerly Wills & Hepworth Ltd) 1972
Printed in England

The world of radio

Today, radio is part of our everyday life, yet only at the beginning of this century it was a miracle. It is still something to marvel at—and a fascinating subject to study.

With this book you will learn, stage by stage, how to build more than one simple receiver. Everything you should know is explained simply and illustrated clearly, and you will have the pleasure of constructing something marvellous that really works.

All the components used are easily available, usually from your local radio dealer. Most large towns have shops specialising in stocking components, but it is also very easy to obtain any you need by post. All the popular electronic construction magazines contain advertisements for mail order supplies. Many of these suppliers provide catalogues which list all the components you will need.

0 7214 0324 7

Radio reception

Radio waves cannot be seen or heard. They are *electro-magnetic* waves, and they flow backwards and forwards (*oscillate*). Each backward and forward movement is known as a *cycle*. The rate of this backward and forward movement (*oscillation*) is known as the frequency of the wave.

A radio wave is also a *carrier* wave. It can 'carry' an electro-magnetic wave of a frequency exactly similar to the sound waves of the speech or music which is being transmitted. This frequency, which is imposed on the carrier wave, is known as an *audio* frequency. It is this electro-magnetic *audio frequency* that a radio receiver translates into sound via the loudspeaker. For a more detailed explanation of this, you might like to read pages 20-26 of the Ladybird book: 'How it Works—Television'.

When radio waves carrying an audio frequency arrive at a receiver, three things happen:

1. *TUNING*. The radio frequency carrier wave is picked up by the aerial. Along this same aerial pass the radio frequency carrier waves from many other transmitting stations, but the signal we want from a particular transmitter must be selected (tuned) from them.

2. *DETECTION*. The next stage is the detection stage, in which the electro-magnetic audio frequency wave is detected from the carrier wave.

3. *AMPLIFICATION*. The electro-magnetic audio signal wave is amplified, or made bigger, and translated from an electrical signal into SOUND by the loud-speaker, from which we hear a reproduction of the transmitted sound.

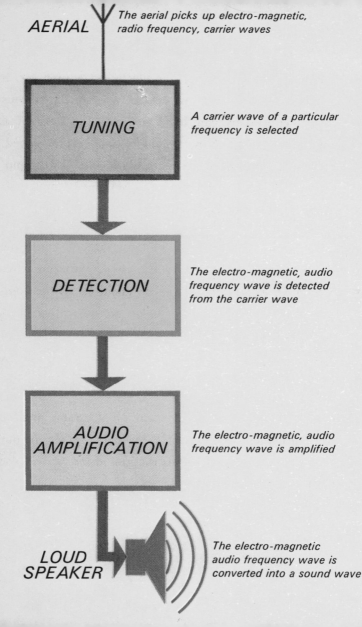

AERIAL
The aerial picks up electro-magnetic, radio frequency, carrier waves

TUNING
A carrier wave of a particular frequency is selected

DETECTION
The electro-magnetic, audio frequency wave is detected from the carrier wave

AUDIO AMPLIFICATION
The electro-magnetic, audio frequency wave is amplified

LOUD SPEAKER
The electro-magnetic audio frequency wave is converted into a sound wave

Reading circuit diagrams

Before building a piece of electronic equipment, a constructor needs to know how to wire up the various components. This can be done with the help of a diagram showing how the components are joined. Electronic engineers have developed a 'shorthand' method of showing the various components and their joining wires. This is the *circuit diagram*.

A circuit diagram is like a map. All the electronic components have symbols, and the connecting wires are shown as straight lines. The positions of the components on the circuit diagram do not normally correspond to their *actual* positions in the completed equipment. Sometimes a *layout diagram* is also used to show where to position the components on a base board.

Many symbols are used in circuit diagrams and we will learn them as we meet them in the course of our construction. To make construction easier we will use both circuit and layout diagrams.

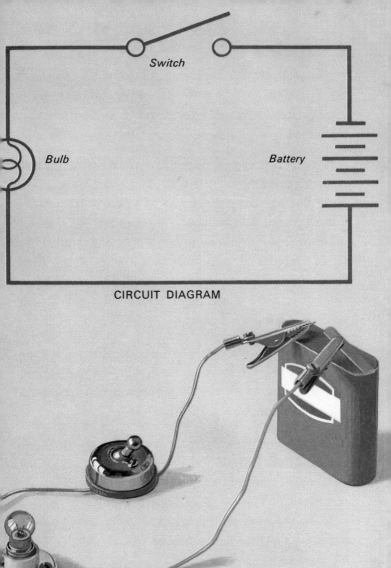

Switch

Bulb

Battery

CIRCUIT DIAGRAM

LAYOUT DIAGRAM

A crystal set – the tuned circuit

A crystal set, the simplest form of radio receiver, is the first stage of our radio. It can operate entirely on its own as a radio receiver, even if no further stages are added.

As we have read on page 6, an aerial picks up all the radio signals (the radio frequency carrier waves) in its path. But we need only signals of a certain frequency— those sent out by a particular transmitter. We therefore need some sort of filter—to allow only one radio station to be received at once. A *tuned circuit* is this filter, because it can be tuned to any frequency we want, and can select one of the many radio frequency carrier waves reaching the aerial.

A tuned circuit consists of a *coil* of wire and a *tuning capacitor*. On the opposite page you can see a circuit diagram for a tuned circuit, and beneath are shown the actual components—a *coil* and *tuning capacitor*.

The particular radio frequency waves which a tuned circuit selects depends on the number of turns of wire on the coil and the 'value' of the capacitor. Since it is inconvenient to keep changing the number of turns of wire on the coil, the capacitor is made with movable plates so that the tuning can be varied and the signals we want selected.

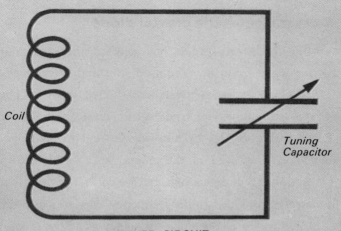

Coil

Tuning
Capacitor

A TUNED CIRCUIT

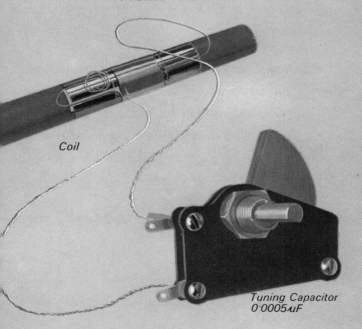

Coil

Tuning Capacitor
0·0005μF

A crystal set – the crystal diode

After the tuned circuit has selected the particular carrier wave frequency required, the audio frequency signal which it carries must be extracted from it. The *crystal* (sometimes referred to as a *diode*) is a simple device that does this by allowing current to pass only one way. It is used in the crystal set as a 'detector'. The action is a complex one, but we can simply say that it detects from the radio frequency carrier wave the *electrical* waves of the same frequency as sound (*audio*) waves and which a loudspeaker or headphone can convert into *sound*.

On the opposite page you will see a circuit diagram showing the tuned circuit mentioned on the previous page but with the symbols for the diode and the earpiece included. With the addition of the aerial and earth symbols, we now have a circuit diagram for a complete working radio set.

Also illustrated are a typical earpiece and a crystal diode.

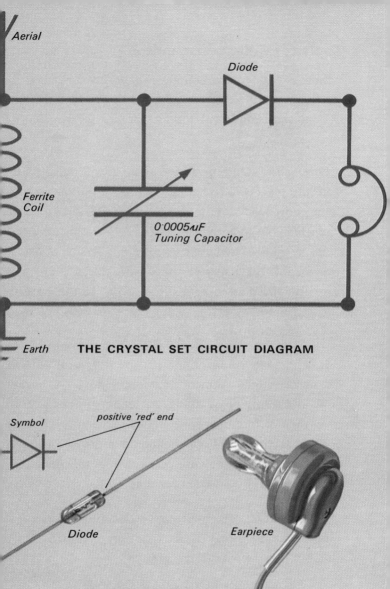

Aerial

Diode

Ferrite
Coil

0·0005uF
Tuning Capacitor

Earth

THE CRYSTAL SET CIRCUIT DIAGRAM

Symbol

positive 'red' end

Diode

Earpiece

Tools for radio construction

Simple radio construction, of the sort described in this book, requires few tools. Most of these can be found in a normal household toolbox or are inexpensive to buy.

During the building of the radio, wires have to be bent into place and sometimes cut to the correct length. Some components are joined by P.V.C. covered copper wire which has to be cut to size and its covering removed from the ends to make the connection. The most useful tool for this is a pair of pointed-nose pliers. These will also strip the plastic from the wire before the connections are made. A pair of wire cutters may also be used to cut and strip wire.

It is possible to buy an inexpensive little tool called a 'wire-cutter and stripper' to do both jobs. A pocket knife is useful for scraping the ends of the wire to clean them before the connections are made. Sandpaper or the rough edge of a matchbox can also be used to clean wires before they are connected. A medium-sized screwdriver will be needed for making the connections.

This radio is to be built on a wooden base, so a few simple woodworking tools—handsaw, gimlet, brace and bit—are also required.

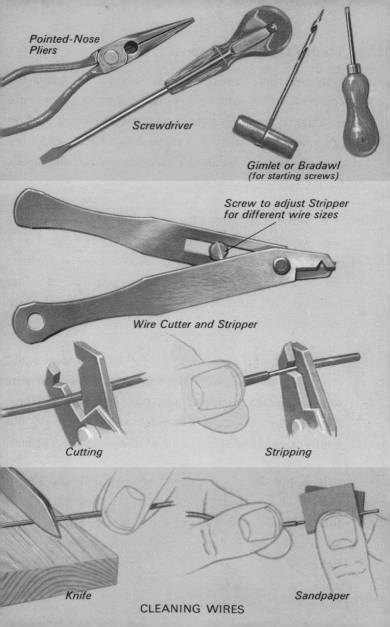

Pointed-Nose Pliers

Screwdriver

Gimlet or Bradawl
(for starting screws)

Screw to adjust Stripper
for different wire sizes

Wire Cutter and Stripper

Cutting

Stripping

Knife

Sandpaper

CLEANING WIRES

Fixing the components

In electronic construction it is usual to *solder* the components into their places in the circuit. This radio is designed for the beginner, so a non-soldering method of connection is used. For those who wish to solder the connections, the technique is explained on the inside back covers of this book.

A simple method of connecting the components uses woodscrews and washers. The screws are No. 6 brass countersunk, half inch screws and the washers are No. 6 brass screwcups. Two dozen of each are required. All are obtainable from your local iron-monger.

The method is explained in the diagram opposite, but remember the following tips: (1) Make sure the wire to be connected is scraped clean until it shines. (2) Where several wires are trapped under one washer, do not finally tighten the screw until all the wires are in place.

It is possible to test a connection with the simple battery and bulb arrangement in the diagram. Touch the two leads onto some of the bare wire either side of the connection. If the connection is good, the bulb will light up.

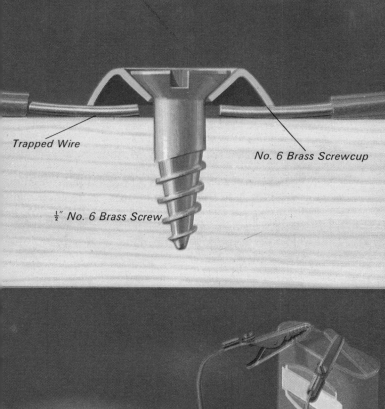

Trapped Wire

No. 6 Brass Screwcup

½" No. 6 Brass Screw

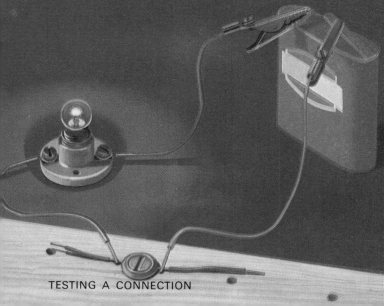

TESTING A CONNECTION

Making the circuit board

In the early days of radio, receivers were made on a baseboard sometimes called a 'bread board'. We are using a form of bread board mounting.

Softwood is used for the base. Mount the screws and screwcups, used for connections, at one inch intervals in two rows of eight. The rows should be an inch-and-a-half apart. This is shown in the drawing facing this page. The two large holes are made with a brace and bit and are for mounting the control components.

The accuracy of the measurements is not vitally important, but it would be helpful to follow those given as closely as possible. Not all the screws are used in building the first part of the radio; the additional screws are needed later as the radio is completed. Although this board is very simple to make, it is important to try to get the screws in straight so that the screwcups press firmly onto the wires.

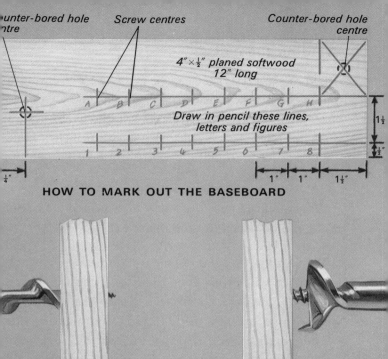

Counter-bored hole centre — Screw centres — Counter-bored hole centre

$4'' \times \frac{1}{2}''$ planed softwood
12" long

Draw in pencil these lines, letters and figures

A B C D E F G H

1 2 3 4 5 6 7 8

$1\frac{1}{2}''$
$\frac{1}{2}''$

$\frac{1}{4}''$

1" 1" $1\frac{1}{2}''$

HOW TO MARK OUT THE BASEBOARD

With a $\frac{3}{8}''$ bit, drill from the marked side
until the point of the bit just appears on
the other side. (Do not drill right through)

With a $\frac{3}{4}''$ bit, drill from the other
side, half way through the board

MAKING THE HOLES

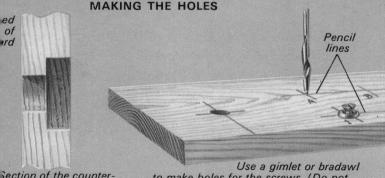

Section of the counter-bored holes

Pencil lines

Use a gimlet or bradawl
to make holes for the screws. (Do not
fully tighten the screws at this stage)

Winding the coil

Before the crystal set can be built, we must wind a tuning coil for the tuned circuit. This is done on a piece of $\frac{3}{8}$ inch diameter ferrite rod. Ferrite is iron dust stuck together. Usually ferrite rods are 6 inches long, so cut a notch all round the centre and smartiy snap the rod in half (Figs. 1 and 2).

Wrap about $1\frac{1}{2}$ inches of sticky tape around the centre of the rod on which to wind the coil (Fig. 3).

Obtain some 36 s.w.g. (standard wire gauge) enamelled copper wire from your radio or electrical dealer. Leaving about 3 inches of wire, secure one end of the wire with sticky tape (Fig. 4) and wind 5 turns, side by side, onto the rod (Fig. 5). Pull out a 3 inch loop and twist the wire until it is tight up to the rod (Fig. 6). Then wind a further 45 turns, side by side, securing the final end with tape. The whole coil can be covered with tape to keep the windings secure.

Remember to leave about 3 inches of spare wire at both ends and at the twisted wire (the 'tapping' point). Later the enamel must be scraped off so that connections can be made.

The illustrations opposite will guide you through each stage.

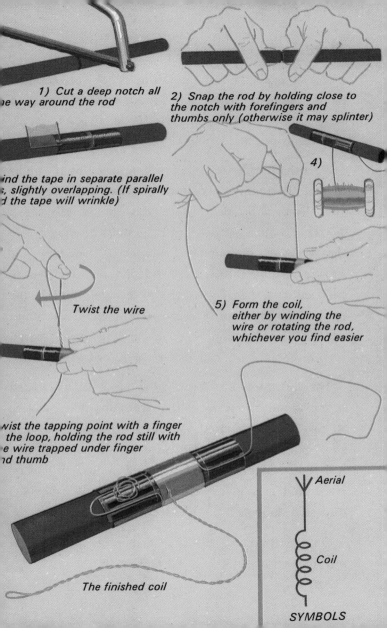

1) Cut a deep notch all
the way around the rod

2) Snap the rod by holding close to
the notch with forefingers and
thumbs only (otherwise it may splinter)

Wind the tape in separate parallel
strips, slightly overlapping. (If spirally
wound the tape will wrinkle)

4)

Twist the wire

5) Form the coil,
either by winding the
wire or rotating the rod,
whichever you find easier

Twist the tapping point with a finger
in the loop, holding the rod still with
the wire trapped under finger
and thumb

The finished coil

Aerial

Coil

SYMBOLS

Building the crystal set

Having made the coil, the ferrite rod can be mounted on the baseboard by twisting a loop of stiff wire around each end and screwing the wire under two screwcups, as shown opposite.

Next the tuned circuit can be completed by the addition of the tuning capacitor. You can buy one from your local radio dealer and you should ask for a $0.0005\mu F$ solid dielectric type. The illustration opposite shows how it is mounted on the baseboard, the capacitor spindle passing through the $\frac{3}{8}$ inch hole. The wiring connections are made to the two terminal nuts on the back of the capacitor. The connecting wire used should be PVC covered copper wire, the ends being bared before they are trapped under the screwcups.

The illustration also shows how the diode is included in the circuit by means of the screwcups. The earpiece is also shown inserted. When purchasing this, you should ask for a crystal earpiece. A pair of high resistance headphones could be used in place of an earpiece, and may give even better results. *Resistance* is discussed on page 32, in the section headed 'Resistors'.

On the following two pages there is some useful information about the aerial and earth.

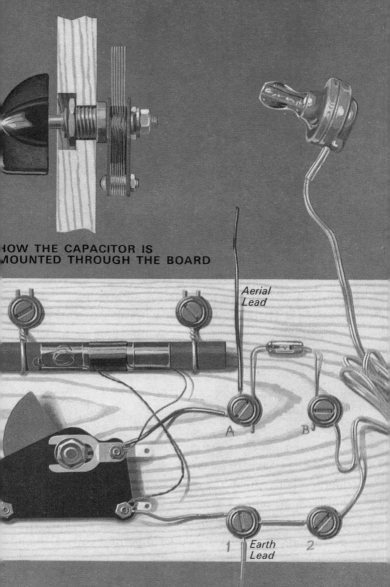

HOW THE CAPACITOR IS
MOUNTED THROUGH THE BOARD

Aerial
Lead

A

B

1

Earth
Lead

2

THE COMPLETED CRYSTAL SET

The crystal set – its aerial and earth

The aerial is the part of the receiver which 'picks up' the radio signals. Unlike our crystal set, many modern transistor radios are sufficiently sensitive to pick up enough signal from the ferrite core of the tuning coil. Although the final radio which we will make will not need an aerial and earth, the crystal set relies on the electrical current set up between a good aerial and earth to work well.

A suitable aerial can be made from inexpensive PVC covered copper wire. The idea is to suspend as much of this wire as possible, as high as possible. The far end can be attached to a tree, the top of a pole or even the eaves of a friendly neighbour's house, but this can be dangerous and is best done by an adult or under the supervision of an adult. The wire should be fastened onto a large screw eye or hook. The near end of the wire may be taken in the top of an upstairs window and connected to the aerial connection on our radio.

For the aerial to be effective, the other side of the tuned circuit has to be connected to earth. The simplest method is to attach the earth lead to the nearest household water pipe. These pipes lead to the ground. If your water pipes are plastic, make your own earth by driving about a yard of copper pipe into soft earth and connecting the earth wire to the top.

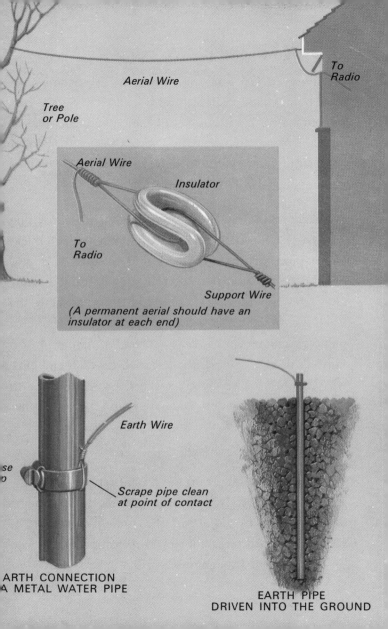

Aerial Wire

Tree
or Pole

To
Radio

Aerial Wire

Insulator

To
Radio

Support Wire

*(A permanent aerial should have an
insulator at each end)*

Earth Wire

Scrape pipe clean
at point of contact

EARTH CONNECTION
A METAL WATER PIPE

EARTH PIPE
DRIVEN INTO THE GROUND

An experimental P.O.W. radio

During the last war, some prisoners in prison camps used home-made radios to keep in touch with events in their native lands. Often, all the components had to be made from items picked up within the camp. Diodes were almost impossible to obtain, so several ingenious home-made alternatives were tried.

The diagram shows one simple method of improvising a diode. Take a small piece of wood, about 1 inch thick, and a piece of washed coke about the size of a pea. Mount the coke on the wood as shown, using a screw and screwcup, and taking a lead from beneath the screwcup. Wind about a foot of steel wire—a length of piano or guitar wire is ideal—around a number 4 or 6 knitting needle, leaving about 1 inch on each end. The wire should now be slightly springy. Fasten one end to the board with a screw and screwcup, taking another lead from this screwcup. Stretch the wire until the free end lightly touches the coke.

Remove the diode from the crystal set and screw the wires in its place. It should be possible to hear some local stations by adjusting the tuning capacitor. If nothing is heard, keep moving the position of the wire on the coke until a signal is heard.

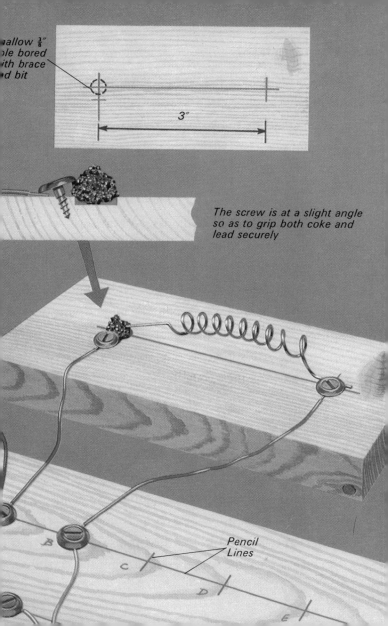

shallow ⅜″
hole bored
with brace
and bit

3″

The screw is at a slight angle
so as to grip both coke and
lead securely

Pencil
Lines

B

C

D

E

The transistor

To most people the word TRANSISTOR means a small radio set, but a transistor is really a single electronic component. The transistor is one of the most important inventions of the last 25 years. It has helped to make electronic equipment smaller and less dependent upon high voltages.

A transistor is like two diodes working together inside one case. Most transistors have three leads, emitter, collector and base. A transistor can be damaged unless the correct leads are used when connecting it into a circuit. The base lead is usually the middle wire and the collector lead is set slightly apart from the other two wires. The transistors we are to use also have a red spot painted on the casing to indicate the collector lead.

We shall be using transistors as amplifiers; that is, to make electrical signals stronger. Transistors are designed so that a small, changing current between the base and emitter produces a large current change between the collector and the emitter. So small signals applied to the base will appear amplified (or made bigger) at the collector. Our first transistor will be used to make louder the sound coming from the crystal set.

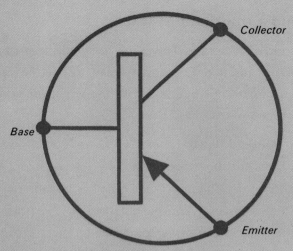

THE SYMBOL FOR A TRANSISTOR

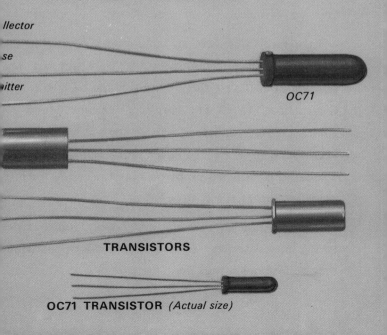

TRANSISTORS

OC71 TRANSISTOR *(Actual size)*

Adding a transistor

The circuit diagram shows how a simple transistor amplifier is inserted where previously we had the earpiece. Compare this diagram with the circuit diagram of the crystal set on page 23.

The transistor used is an OC71, and other extra components for this stage are a 2·7K resistor and a 9-volt battery. The battery is the small transistor radio type PP3, for which can be obtained an inexpensive snap connector. Resistors are discussed on the next page. This resistor forms an output 'load' for the collector, and the earpiece is connected across the resistor.

Take care to connect up the circuit as shown in the drawing. The connections of the transistor are important. Join the emitter to screw 5, the base to E and the collector to F. The earpiece is removed and re-connected to F and G. Connect the red battery connector lead to screw 5, and the black lead to screw G. The radio is switched on by pushing the connector into place on top of the battery.

This one transistor should make a big improvement to the crystal set; the same stations will be heard but they will be much louder.

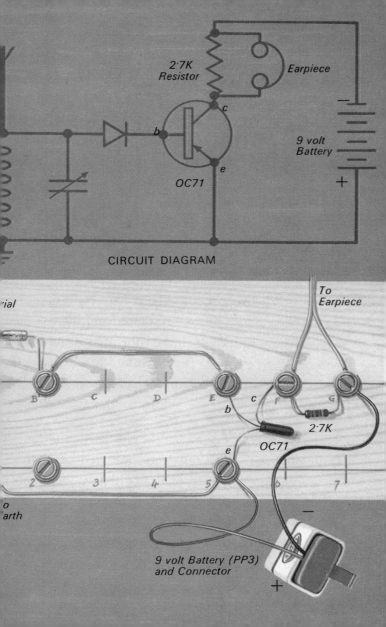

2·7K
Resistor

Earpiece

c

9 volt
Battery

b

e

OC71

+

CIRCUIT DIAGRAM

To
Earpiece

rial

B C D E

b c F G

OC71 2·7K

e

2 3 4 5 6 7

o
arth

9 volt Battery (PP3)
and Connector

−

+

Resistors

Resistors are very common components in electronic construction. Look at most pieces of equipment and you will see several small, wire-ended tubes with brightly coloured bands. These are called resistors because they 'resist' the flow of electrical current in the circuit. This is done to adjust the voltages and flow of current at various places in a circuit.

The little tubes are filled with a carbon composition, and the coloured bands give the *value* of the resistor. This value is called the *resistance* and is measured in *ohms*. When one knows the colour code opposite, it is easy to work out the resistance from the coloured bands. The tolerance of the resistor, that is, how close one can expect it to be to the value, is sometimes indicated with another coloured band. Our radio can use resistors of any tolerance, so this band may be ignored.

The symbol for resistance is the Greek letter omega Ω. Quite often, very high resistances are used—sometimes thousands or millions of ohms. To reduce the number of noughts, we call thousands K Ω (Kilo ohms) and millions M Ω (or Mega ohms). The ohm sign is usually omitted from circuit diagrams when the Kilo (K) and Mega (M) signs are used.

THE SYMBOL FOR A RESISTOR

First Number
Second Number
Number of Noughts
Tolerance Band

RESISTOR COLOUR SCOPE

ACK	0 (or 0 noughts)	GREEN	5 (or 5 noughts)
OWN	1 (or 1 nought)	BLUE	6 (or 6 noughts)
ED	2 (or 2 noughts)	VIOLET	7 (or 7 noughts)
ANGE	3 (or 3 noughts)	GREY	8 (or 8 noughts)
LOW	4 (or 4 noughts)	WHITE	9 (or 9 noughts)

TOLERANCE COLOURS

GOLD 5%	SILVER 10%	SALMON 20%

BROWN, BLACK, BROWN
100

YELLOW, VIOLET, ORANGE
=47000 or 47k

Biasing the transistor

The transistor amplifier we have built is the simplest arrangement possible. If a transistor is to be used efficiently, one has to supply the correct voltages to its various parts; this is called *biasing*. In our simple arrangement the signal from the diode provided a voltage to *bias* the base of the transistor. Resistors can be added to make the biasing correct.

The circuit shows how the transistor is biased with two resistors. (33K Ω—orange, orange, orange, and 150K Ω—brown, green, yellow.) They give the correct voltages between the collector, base and emitter. Take care to connect the resistors in the places shown or the effect will be ruined.

This addition to the radio will not increase the volume in any noticeable way, but the biasing is essential before the next stage is added.

The wire ends of resistors, like any other components, can become dirty and greasy, so scrape the wires clean before screwing them into place.

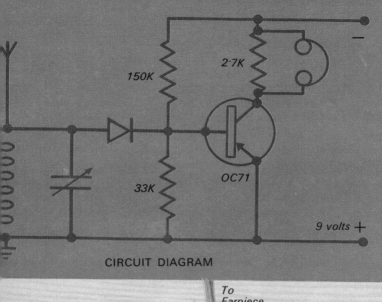

CIRCUIT DIAGRAM

150K

2·7K

33K

OC71

9 volts +

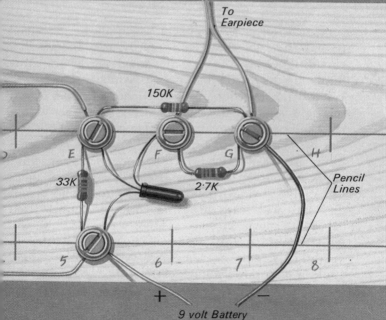

To Earpiece

150K

E

F

G

H

33K

2·7K

Pencil Lines

5

6

7

8

+

−

9 volt Battery

Adding a second transistor

Before we can add another transistor to our radio, two new components must be introduced—a *potentiometer* and a *capacitor*.

The potentiometer is a variable resistance. Look at the drawing on the opposite page and you will see that it has three contacts. The outer two are each end of a circular carbon track. The centre tag is joined to a movable contact which slides over the track when the shaft is rotated. By moving the shaft, which is usually fitted with a plastic knob, any part of the resistance can be used and tapped off through the centre tag. Potentiometers are often used, as in this case, as volume controls.

A *capacitor* is a component which allows the signal to pass but not the fixed voltages used to power a circuit. It consists of two plates which are separated by insulating material; the circuit symbol shows this. Electrolytic capacitors must be connected into a circuit the right way round. One end is marked either with a red band or a + sign, and this side goes to the positive side of the circuit. The negative (—) wire is connected to the metal can which forms the body of the capacitor, and which may be marked with a black band. Sometimes this is not obvious, but follow the circuit and layout diagrams with care to avoid mistakes. Other fixed capacitors can be connected either way round: we will meet these later. The value of capacity is written in microfarads, (µF or sometimes MFD). We require 10µF at a working voltage of 16-volts.

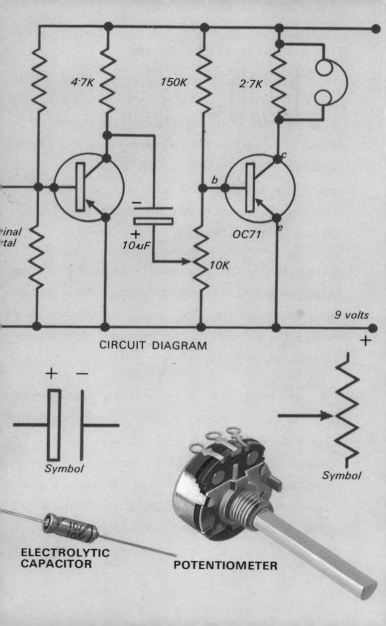

4·7K

150K

2·7K

b

c

e

OC71

─
+
10µF

10K

inal
tal

9 volts
+

CIRCUIT DIAGRAM

+   ─

Symbol

Symbol

ELECTROLYTIC
CAPACITOR

POTENTIOMETER

The second transistor stage

The circuit for the second stage is shown on the previous page. The signal is taken from the collector of our first transistor, through the capacitor to the sliding contact of the volume control potentiometer. The nearer the centre contact is adjusted to the base side of the control, the more signal is allowed to go to the base of the second transistor. The greater the signal reaching this transistor, the louder will be its output.

The potentiometer is mounted in the spare $\frac{3}{8}$ inch hole. Its tags are too close together to use the large screwcups, so small screws are used. These are screwed down through the holes in the potentiometer tags, trapping the leads under the tags.

Remove the 2·7K resistor from F and G and connect in the new components carefully, following the layout diagram facing this page. As you work, compare the layout diagram, connection by connection, with the circuit diagram. This additional transistor will greatly increase the volume, enough to drive a loudspeaker, which is the next addition.

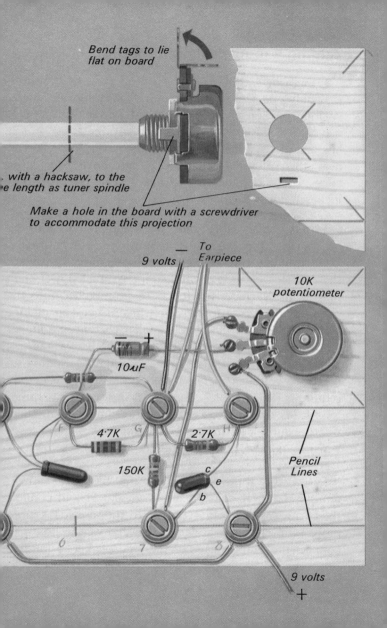

Bend tags to lie
flat on board

... with a hacksaw, to the
... e length as tuner spindle

Make a hole in the board with a screwdriver
to accommodate this projection

9 volts

To
Earpiece

10K
potentiometer

$10\mu F$

4·7K

2·7K

150K

c

e

b

F

G

H

Pencil
Lines

6

7

8

9 volts

Adding a loudspeaker

Using our radio with an earpiece means, of course, that only one person at a time can hear the programme. A loudspeaker changes electrical waves into sound waves in the same way that an earpiece does, but it has a large cardboard cone so that several people can hear the sound. Loudspeakers can have very large cones, but a smaller cone speaker with a diameter of 3 inches is ideal for our purpose.

Loudspeakers are made with inputs of varying resistances, and our radio requires a 3 or 5 Ω type. Unfortunately the loudspeaker cannot directly replace the earpiece because its resistance is much lower than that of the earpiece, so it has to be matched into the circuit with a *transformer*. A transformer can change a current of one voltage to a smaller current of a higher voltage or to a larger current of a smaller voltage. It consists of a 'primary' and 'secondary' winding of fine wire round a metal 'former'. The transformer we require is the Eagle LT700. This transformer has rather long leads, and these may be shortened by winding them tightly round a knitting needle. This makes spiral leads which can then be pulled out to reach the screws.

Screw the transformer onto the base, as shown; remove the 2·7K resistor across G and H and connect the correct leads (colour coded) to the screwcups. Two more screwcups are added at the end of the board to connect the output leads to the loudspeaker, using two small crocodile clips.

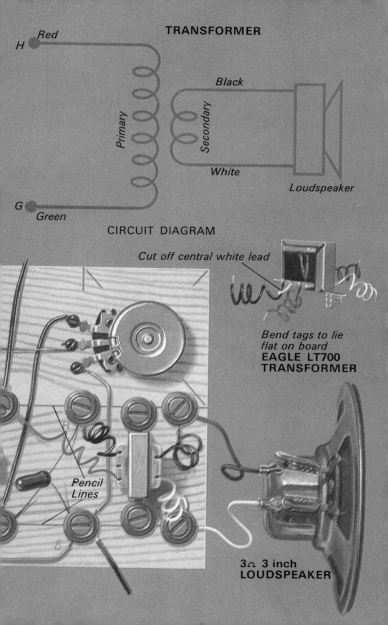

TRANSFORMER

H ○ Red

Primary

G ○ Green

Black

Secondary

White

Loudspeaker

CIRCUIT DIAGRAM

Cut off central white lead

Bend tags to lie flat on board
EAGLE LT700 TRANSFORMER

Pencil Lines

3Ω 3 inch LOUDSPEAKER

Regeneration

We shall now replace our simple crystal set stage with a transistor stage, using *regeneration*. Regeneration will enable our first transistor in the radio to be used three times.

The circuit shows the regeneration stage. The signal from the aerial is tuned by the coil and variable capacitor, the orange marked signal then passes through capacitor C1 to be amplified by the transistor and appear at a *radio frequency choke* (R.F.C.). Part of this signal, marked in blue, passes through C2 to a pair of diodes which change the radio signal into an audio signal, which is amplified again by the transistor. The signal, now marked red, passes through C3 back to the coil. The part of the coil tapped between the transistor collector (through C1) and earth, allows the signal to reach the collector again.

This means that some of the signal at R.F.C. has been amplified three times, so this is a very economical use of one transistor. Passing signals back again like this is called *feedback*. If the feedback is too great, the circuit will produce a howling sound, so C3 is an adjustable capacitor to control the amount of feedback. The final signal is taken from R.F.C. through capacitor C4.

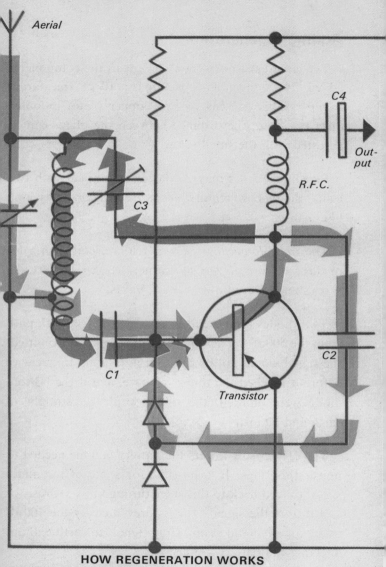

Aerial

C3

C4

Output

R.F.C.

C1

C2

Transistor

HOW REGENERATION WORKS

rcuit diagrams, wires which cross one another, (but do NOT touch and
NOT connected), are sometimes shown like this ┿ (as in the diagram)
e this ─┴─. Shown like this ─●─ always means they are connected.

Adding regeneration

The circuit shows the new stage with the components added. The adjustable capacitor is a 10 pF (picafarad) *trimmer*. This consists of two copper plates mounted on a pot base; the distance between the plates can be adjusted with the small screw.

Fixed capacitors may be flat or cylindrical with two leads; the type we require, *ceramic capacitors*, may look like a disc.

The *radio frequency choke* is really a coil with a lot of turns of wire on a small former. The choke acts like a resistance to radio-frequency waves.

Two diodes are needed to provide the feedback path from the 500pF capacitor. If the top diode were omitted, the signal would not be changed into audio frequencies before it reached the transistor base, and if the bottom diode were omitted, the signal would go straight to earth and be lost.

The 1K resistor lowers the battery voltage needed to power this stage. It is possible for some of the audio signal to feed back to this stage through this 1K resistor and distort the signal. This is prevented by the 100μF capacitor which takes any stray signals to earth without affecting the battery voltage.

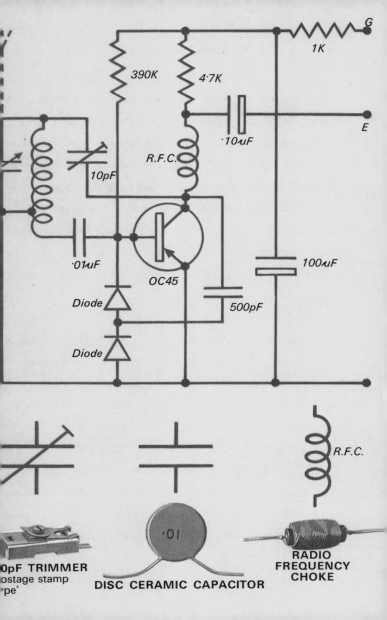

390K

4·7K

1K

G

·10μF

E

R.F.C.

10pF

·01μF

OC45

Diode

Diode

500pF

100μF

10pF TRIMMER
'postage stamp
type'

DISC CERAMIC CAPACITOR

·01

R.F.C.

RADIO
FREQUENCY
CHOKE

Wiring the regeneration stage

The drawing shows how this stage is wired onto the board. Before wiring the stage, all the components from the crystal stage, up to screws E and 5, are removed except for the coil and tuning capacitor. The diode is removed to become one of the two diodes in the new stage. Follow the drawing carefully, adding one component at a time and checking its position on the circuit diagram. There are many bare wires which come close to each other, and great care must be taken to ensure they do not touch each other. The 1K resistor must not touch screws E and F.

The trimmer is trapped by its tags under screws A and B; if it is too long or too short, the screws may be moved. All three connections to the coil are now used, and if the wires are not placed in the correct positions, regeneration will not occur. The drawing shows how to place these three wires. The 10µF capacitor takes the signal from the new stage to the base of the next OC71 transistor. The advantage of this new stage is that our radio will have a greater output and no longer need a large aerial and an earth. Regeneration is tricky to get used to, but once mastered, the results are surprising.

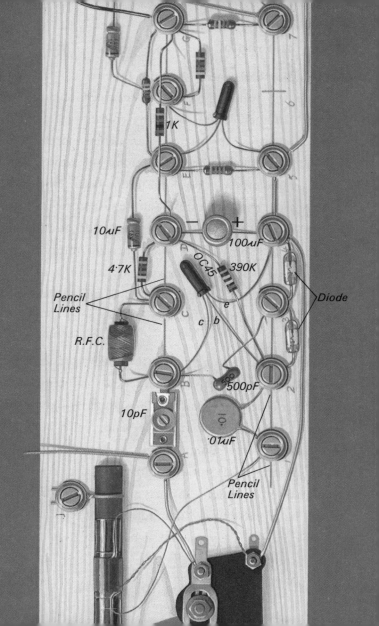

1K

10µF

100µF

4·7K

OC45

390K

Pencil
Lines

Diode

e

c   b

R.F.C.

10pF

500pF

·01µF

Pencil
Lines

Using the radio

Operating a regenerative radio requires care at first because the trimmer has to be adjusted to suit the strength of each signal. Begin by connecting about 3 yards of wire to the radio as an aerial; no earth is required. Set the tuning capacitor about midway and screw in the trimmer until the radio begins to howl. Unscrew the trimmer until the noise just stops, and try to tune in a station. The trimmer should then be adjusted until it is just short of the point when the radio howls. The general method for receiving any station is to tune it in with the tuning capacitor and to adjust the feed-back trimmer until the howling just disappears.

The feedback not only makes the radio more sensitive but also the tuning becomes sharper, so the tuning knob must be rotated very slowly. This sensitivity makes the radio ideal for the medium wave band, which is rather overcrowded. The tuning should be sharp enough to tune in individual stations without the background sounds of other stations. In areas of good signal strength, it will be possible to use the radio without an aerial at all, merely relying upon the signal picked up by the ferrite rod coil.

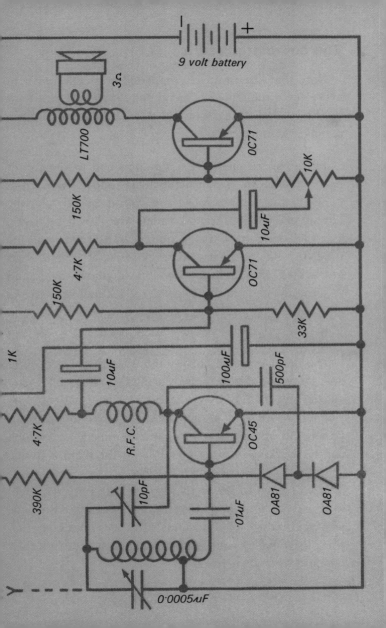

The completed radio

Now that the radio is completed, you may wish to make the circuit board into a simple case. The circuit board is used as a front panel, and end and bottom panels are added.

These can be made from similar wood to the circuit board (4 inch by $\frac{1}{2}$ inch planed softwood). The bottom panel is the same size as the circuit board and the measurements for the end panels are shown opposite. The end panel next to the output transformer may be used to hold the loudspeaker. A series of $\frac{3}{8}$ inch holes are drilled with a brace and bit to allow the sound to leave the case, and the speaker is secured with screws and cups. The panels are joined with panel pins and glue.

The battery may be firmly mounted above screws D and E on the circuit board, using $2\frac{1}{2}$ inches of $\frac{1}{4}$ inch elastic and two screws and cups. Two smart plastic pointer knobs and a tuning scale complete the front panel. The tuning scale is a paper gummed label which can be marked with the positions of the main stations.

If you have followed these pages carefully, you will now have a useful working radio. You will also have shared the thrill of thousands of other radio constructors, listening to sounds coming from a radio receiver which is your own work.

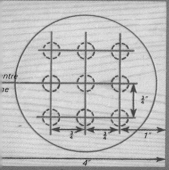

How to mark out the position of the Loudspeaker and $\frac{3}{8}''$ holes

The Loudspeaker is mounted over the circle with 4 screws and cups

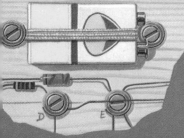

The Battery is mounted above screws D and E

THE COMPLETED RADIO

Contents